AF693151

Computer Application In Business (Concise Notes)

NotesKaro

Published by NotesKaro Inc, 2025.

COMPUTER APPLICATION IN BUSINESS (CONCISE NOTES)

First edition. May 22, 2025.

ISBN: 979-8231305650

Written by NotesKaro.

Table of Contents

Unit 1: Introduction to Computer

1. WHAT IS A COMPUTER? A computer is an advanced electronic machine that takes raw data as input, processes it under a set of instructions (called a program), and delivers meaningful output. It can perform a wide range of tasks with incredible speed and accuracy, making it indispensable in every sector from education to multinational businesses.

Example: If you book a train ticket online, you input your travel details into a website (input), the system checks availability and processes payment (processing), and finally shows your ticket (output).

2. Characteristics of Computers

- **Speed:** A modern computer can execute millions of instructions per second. For example, a bank transaction across continents takes mere seconds.

- **Accuracy:** It performs operations with almost zero error. For example, accounting software calculates complex taxes with precision.

- **Automation:** Once instructions are set, it works without interruption.

- **Storage:** Computers can store terabytes of data (1 TB = 1024 GB). For example, Google's servers store zettabytes of data.

- **Versatility:** Same device can run a game, a spreadsheet, and a design tool.

- **Multitasking:** Can run multiple programs simultaneously.

- **Diligence:** Unlike humans, computers don't get tired or distracted.

3. Components of a Computer System

- **Hardware:** Tangible parts like CPU, monitor, keyboard.
- **Software:** Programs that run the hardware. Divided into system, application, and utility software.
- **User:** Operator of the system (humans or even another machine).
- **Data:** Information processed and stored by the system.

4. Types of Computers

• **Analog Computers:** Handle physical values like speed, temperature.

• **Digital Computers:** Most common; deal in binary (0s and 1s).

• **Hybrid Computers:** Used in hospitals and research labs — combines both analog and digital features.

REAL EXAMPLE: A hybrid computer is used in ICUs where patient's temperature (analog) is monitored and converted into digital data for further processing.

5. Generations of Computers | Generation | Technology | Example | Features | |————————|————————|——————|———————| | First | Vacuum Tubes | ENIAC | Very large, slow | | Second | Transistors | IBM 1401 | Faster, smaller | | Third | IC (Integrated Circuit) | IBM 360 | Compact, multitasking | | Fourth | Microprocessors | Personal Computers | Very fast, portable | | Fifth | AI & Quantum | Smart assistants, ChatGPT | Intelligent systems |

6. Classification Based on Size

- **Microcomputers:** Used in homes and offices (Laptops, Desktops).
- **Minicomputers:** Used by small to mid-level organizations.
- **Mainframe Computers:** Large-scale usage in banks, insurance companies.
- **Supercomputers:** Used in weather forecasting, space research.

7. Input, Output, Processing, and Storage Devices

- **Input Devices:** Mouse, Keyboard, Scanner, Touchscreen, Webcam, Microphone.

- **Output Devices:** Monitor, Printer, Projector, Headphones.

- **Processing Devices:** CPU (includes ALU – Arithmetic Logic Unit, and CU – Control Unit).

- **Storage Devices:**

  ○ **Primary Storage:** RAM, ROM

  ○ **Secondary Storage:** HDD, SSD, USB drives, Optical Disks

  ○ **Cloud Storage:** Google Drive, OneDrive (remote storage)

8. MEMORY CONCEPTS | Memory Type | Use | Volatile? | Speed | |————————-|——-|————————-|——————| | RAM | Temporary work memory | Yes | Very fast | | ROM | Startup instructions | No | Fast | | Cache | Holds frequently used data | Yes | Extremely fast | | Virtual Memory | Uses HDD as extension of RAM | Yes | Slower than RAM |

9. Types of Software

- **System Software:** Controls hardware (e.g., Windows, Linux, MacOS)
- **Application Software:** Used for tasks like writing, calculating, editing (e.g., MS Office, Photoshop)
- **Utility Software:** Maintains performance (e.g., Disk Cleanup, Antivirus)
- **Open Source Software:** Free to use and modify (e.g., LibreOffice, GIMP)

EXAMPLE IN BUSINESS: Tally is an application software used for accounting by small and medium businesses in India.

10. Importance of Computers in Business

- **Accounting and Finance:** Automates payroll, expense tracking, tax calculations.
- **Marketing:** Tools like Google Ads and social media platforms help in digital marketing.
- **Inventory Management:** Tracks stock, predicts demand.
- **Customer Support:** Chatbots and CRM software enhance customer service.
- **Communication:** Emails, messaging tools, video conferencing.
- **E-Commerce:** Online portals like Amazon and Flipkart rely fully on computer systems.

CASE STUDY: *Amazon uses powerful supercomputers and AI to analyze consumer data, predict buying patterns, automate warehousing, and provide instant recommendations.*

11. Emerging Trends in Computer Applications

- **AI and Machine Learning:** Chatbots, voice recognition, fraud detection.
- **Cloud Computing:** Reduces need for physical infrastructure.
- **IoT (Internet of Things):** Devices like smartwatches, smart homes.
- **Big Data Analytics:** Helps businesses make data-driven decisions.
- **Cybersecurity:** Essential for protecting digital business assets.
- **Blockchain:** Used in secure digital transactions and logistics.

12. FAQs and Clarifications

- *Q: Can I run a computer without software?*

○ No, software is needed to interact with hardware.

- *Q: Is smartphone a computer?*

○ Yes, it is a microcomputer with touch input and wireless connectivity.

- *Q: Which memory is used during system boot?*

○ ROM (contains BIOS/firmware).

13. SUMMARY / QUICK Recap Computers are fast, accurate, and versatile systems. They consist of hardware and software components that work together to perform various tasks. In business, they serve in financial management, operations, communications, and strategy. Emerging tech like AI, cloud, and IoT are further expanding computer applications.

14. Business Insight Businesses that fail to adopt computer technology often fall behind. A digitally enabled business can scale faster, serve customers better, and adapt quickly to changes in the market.

Unit 2: Operating System and Database Management System (DBMS)

Part A: Operating System (OS)

1. WHAT IS AN OPERATING System? An Operating System (OS) is system software that acts as an interface between a user and the computer hardware. It manages all hardware and software resources and provides a platform for other software to run.

Example: Windows, macOS, Linux, Android.

2. Functions of Operating System

- **Process Management:** Handles creation, execution, and termination of processes.
- **Memory Management:** Allocates and deallocates memory space as required.
- **File Management:** Maintains and controls data files.
- **Device Management:** Manages device communication via drivers.
- **Security & Access Control:** Protects system resources.
- **User Interface:** Provides GUI (Graphical User Interface) or CLI (Command Line Interface).

REAL EXAMPLE: When you open MS Word, OS allocates memory, manages input from keyboard, displays output, and handles saving the file.

---

3. Types of Operating Systems

Type	Description	Examples
Batch OS	Executes batches of jobs without user interaction	Early IBM systems
Time-Sharing OS	Shares system time among multiple users	Unix
Distributed OS	Manages a group of independent computers	LOCUS
Network OS	Manages data over a network	Windows Server
Real-Time OS	Executes real-time tasks immediately	RTLinux, VxWorks
Mobile OS	Designed for smartphones	Android, iOS

4. Common Operating Systems in Business

- **Windows:** Most widely used OS in offices.
- **Linux:** Preferred for servers, security, and open-source flexibility.
- **macOS:** Used in design and publishing industries.
- **Android/iOS:** Used in mobile applications and POS systems.

BUSINESS INSIGHT: A supermarket may use Android OS-based systems at checkout and Linux-based servers for internal operations.

5. User Interfaces in OS

- **GUI (Graphical User Interface):** Easy to use; uses icons and menus. Example: Windows.
- **CLI (Command Line Interface):** Text-based; used by programmers. Example: Linux terminal.
- **TUI (Touch User Interface):** Mobile/tablet-based. Example: Smartphones.

6. Example of OS Use in Business

- Banks use **Unix/Linux** for secure server environments.
- Retail outlets use **Windows POS systems**.
- Tech companies use **macOS** for creative work and **Linux** for backend systems.

Part B: Database Management System (DBMS)

1. WHAT IS DBMS? A Database Management System (DBMS) is software that allows the creation, maintenance, and use of databases. It manages data efficiently and allows users to perform multiple tasks with ease.

Example: MySQL, Oracle, MS Access, PostgreSQL.

2. Functions of DBMS

- **Data Storage & Retrieval:** Efficiently stores and fetches data.
- **Data Manipulation:** Enables adding, updating, deleting data.
- **Data Security:** Restricts unauthorized access.
- **Backup and Recovery:** Prevents data loss.
- **Concurrency Control:** Manages simultaneous access by multiple users.
- **Data Integrity:** Ensures accuracy and consistency of data.

---

3. TYPES OF DBMS

Type	Description	Example
Hierarchical	Data in tree-like structure	IBM IMS
Network	Data organized in graph	CODASYL
Relational (RDBMS)	Data in tables	MySQL, Oracle
Object-Oriented	Data as objects	db4o

4. Advantages of DBMS

- Reduces data redundancy
- Ensures data consistency
- Provides data security
- Increases efficiency
- Supports multi-user access

EXAMPLE IN BUSINESS: A retail store uses MySQL to store product inventory, sales data, and customer information. Staff can access real-time stock levels.

---

5. RDBMS vs DBMS

Feature	DBMS	RDBMS
Structure	File-based	Table-based
Integrity Constraints	Not enforced	Enforced
Multi-user Access	Limited	Supported
Example	MS Access	MySQL, Oracle

---

6. SQL – Structured Query Language SQL is the standard language used to communicate with relational databases.

- **SELECT:** Retrieve data
- **INSERT:** Add data
- **UPDATE:** Modify data
- **DELETE:** Remove data

Example: SELECT * FROM Employees WHERE Department = 'Sales';

7. Cloud-based DBMS

- Examples: Google Firebase, Amazon RDS, Microsoft Azure SQL.
- Allows businesses to scale without maintaining physical servers.
- Enables access to data globally in real-time.

---

8. CASE STUDY: USE of DBMS in E-Commerce Flipkart uses Oracle DBMS for inventory and customer management. It supports high-speed transactions and real-time order tracking. This enhances customer satisfaction and operational efficiency.

---

9. Summary / Recap An **Operating System** ensures smooth interaction between the user and computer by managing memory, processes, and hardware. A **DBMS** helps businesses manage large volumes of data effectively and securely. Both are critical tools in modern digital businesses.

10. FAQs

- *Q: Can a mobile phone have a DBMS?*

○ Yes, apps like WhatsApp use SQLite (a lightweight DBMS) to store messages.

- *Q: Is Excel a DBMS?*

○ No, Excel is a spreadsheet tool. It lacks data integrity and multi-user control.

- *Q: Can I use Linux without a GUI?*

○ Yes, servers often use Linux in command-line mode to save resources.

Unit 3: Computer Networks

1. Introduction to Computer Networks

A COMPUTER NETWORK is a group of interconnected computers that can share resources and information. These connections can be wired (like Ethernet) or wireless (like Wi-Fi).

Example: The internet is the largest example of a computer network.

2. Objectives of Networking

- Resource Sharing (printers, files, applications)
- Data Communication
- Remote Access
- Cost Efficiency
- Scalability & Flexibility

BUSINESS EXAMPLE: Offices use LANs (Local Area Networks) to connect all employee systems to shared servers, printers, and the internet.

3. Types of Computer Networks

Type	Description	Range	Example
LAN	Local Area Network	Within a building	Office, School
MAN	Metropolitan Area Network	City-wide	Cable TV Network
WAN	Wide Area Network	Global	Internet
PAN	Personal Area Network	Very short range	Bluetooth devices

4. Components of Computer Networks

- **Router:** Directs data between networks.
- **Switch:** Connects devices within a LAN.
- **Hub:** Basic device that connects multiple computers.
- **Modem:** Converts digital data into signals for internet.
- **NIC (Network Interface Card):** Hardware to connect a computer to a network.
- **Cables:** Like Ethernet, used for physical connections.

5. Network Topologies

TOPOLOGY REFERS TO the layout of a network. | Topology | Description | Pros | Cons | |——————|—————————-|————|————| | Bus | All devices connected to a single cable | Cheap | Fault in cable brings network down | | Star | All devices connected to a central hub | Easy to manage | Hub failure affects whole network | | Ring | Devices connected in a circular fashion | Equal access | One failure affects the loop | | Mesh | Every device connected to every other | Reliable | Expensive | | Hybrid | Combination of two or more topologies | Flexible | Complex design |

6. Transmission Media

- **Wired Media:**
  - *Twisted Pair Cable:* Cheap, used in LAN.
  - *Coaxial Cable:* Used in TV cable.
  - *Fiber Optic Cable:* High-speed, long-distance.
- **Wireless Media:**
  - *Radio Waves, Microwaves, Infrared*

EXAMPLE: Fiber optics is used by banks for secure, fast transactions.

7. Network Devices

Device	Function
Router	Connects different networks
Switch	Connects devices in a LAN
Hub	Broadcasts data to all devices
Bridge	Connects two networks
Gateway	Connects different protocols
Repeater	Amplifies signal in long networks

8. Internet, Intranet, and Extranet

- **Internet:** Global network of networks.
- **Intranet:** Private network for employees.
- **Extranet:** Intranet extended to partners/vendors.

Example:

- *Internet:* Google
- *Intranet:* Infosys internal portal
- *Extranet:* Amazon's vendor management system

9. Network Protocols

PROTOCOLS ARE RULES for communication. | Protocol | Purpose | |———————|——————-| | HTTP/HTTPS | Web browsing | | FTP | File transfer | | TCP/IP | Core internet communication | | SMTP/POP3 | Email | | DNS | Domain name resolution |

10. Cloud Networking

CLOUD NETWORKING ALLOWS data and applications to be hosted remotely and accessed over the internet.

Example: Google Drive, Microsoft Azure, AWS.

Advantages:

- Cost-effective
- Scalable
- Accessible anywhere
- Disaster recovery

11. Cybersecurity in Networking

SECURING NETWORKS IS essential for protecting data.

- **Firewall:** Filters incoming/outgoing traffic
- **Antivirus:** Detects and removes malware
- **Encryption:** Protects data during transmission
- **VPN:** Secure remote access

Business Case: Banks use end-to-end encryption and multi-factor authentication to protect customer data.

12. Real-Life Use Cases of Computer Networks in Business

- **E-commerce:** Amazon uses WAN to connect its global operations.

- **Online Banking:** Banks use secure networks to manage online transactions.

- **Work-from-home:** VPNs allow employees to securely access office networks remotely.

- **Retail Chains:** McDonald's uses a centralized network to manage orders, billing, and inventory.

13. Summary / Key Takeaways

COMPUTER NETWORKS ENABLE fast, efficient, and secure communication between devices and users. From personal Bluetooth connections to global internet connectivity, networks are essential in modern business operations.

14. FAQs

- *Q: What's the difference between a router and a switch?*

  ○ A router connects different networks; a switch connects devices within the same network.

- *Q: Can a mobile phone be part of a network?*

  ○ Yes, via Wi-Fi, Bluetooth, or mobile data.

- *Q: What is the most secure network type?*

  ○ A private intranet with encryption and firewalls.

Unit 4: Basics of Internet

1. Introduction to Internet

THE INTERNET IS A GLOBAL system of interconnected computer networks that use the standard Internet Protocol Suite (TCP/IP) to communicate between billions of devices.

Example: Websites like Google, YouTube, and Amazon function via the Internet.

2. History of the Internet

- **1960s:** ARPANET developed by the US Department of Defense.
- **1980s:** National Science Foundation Network (NSFNET) established.
- **1990s:** Commercialization of the Internet began.
- **Today:** Billions of devices are connected globally.

3. How the Internet Works

- **Client:** A device that requests data (like a browser).
- **Server:** A device that provides data (like a website).
- **IP Address:** Unique number assigned to each device.
- **DNS (Domain Name System):** Converts domain names (like google.com) into IP addresses.
- **ISP (Internet Service Provider):** Provides Internet access to users.

EXAMPLE: Typing www.amazon.in in a browser sends a request to Amazon's server using DNS, which responds with the web page data.

4. Key Internet Terms

Term	Meaning
WWW	World Wide Web – collection of webpages
URL	Uniform Resource Locator – web address
HTTP/HTTPS	Protocols to access websites securely
HTML	Language used to design web pages
Browser	Software to access the web (Chrome, Firefox)

5. Types of Internet Connections

Type	Description
Dial-up	Slow, uses telephone line
Broadband	Fast, uses DSL/cable
Fiber Optic	High-speed, expensive
Wireless	Wi-Fi, Mobile Data (3G/4G/5G)

EXAMPLE: A business might use a fiber connection for reliability, while a user uses 4G on mobile.

6. Internet Services

- **Email:** Sending/receiving electronic messages.
- **Search Engines:** Google, Bing – to find information.
- **Social Media:** Platforms like Facebook, Instagram.
- **E-commerce:** Online shopping portals like Flipkart.
- **Online Banking:** Secure transactions via bank portals.
- **Cloud Storage:** Services like Google Drive, Dropbox.

7. Advantages of the Internet in Business

- Global communication
- 24/7 customer support via chatbots
- Digital marketing & advertising
- E-commerce and online transactions
- Remote working & video conferencing

EXAMPLE: Zomato uses the internet to connect customers with nearby restaurants and delivery partners.

8. Internet Protocols

- **TCP/IP:** Core communication protocol
- **HTTP/HTTPS:** Web browsing
- **FTP:** File transfer
- **SMTP/POP3:** Email
- **VoIP:** Voice over IP for calling (Zoom, Skype)

9. Cyber Threats on the Internet

- **Phishing:** Fake emails to steal data
- **Malware:** Harmful software
- **Ransomware:** Blocks access until payment is made
- **Data Breaches:** Leak of confidential data
- **Spyware:** Tracks user activities secretly

Preventive Measures:

- Use strong passwords
- Enable 2FA (Two-Factor Authentication)
- Install antivirus software
- Avoid suspicious links/emails

10. Safe Browsing Practices

- Use HTTPS-enabled websites
- Regularly update software
- Don't share personal information
- Logout from sessions
- Use VPN on public networks

BUSINESS TIP: Secure websites build customer trust and protect user data.

11. Internet & E-Governance

GOVERNMENTS USE THE Internet to provide services like:

- Filing taxes (e.g., Income Tax portal)
- Digital payments (e.g., BHIM, UPI)
- Public grievance redressal
- Online voting pilots

Example: Digital India initiative promotes e-governance and rural internet access.

12. Real-Life Applications of Internet in Business

- **Flipkart:** Online product catalog and sales
- **OYO Rooms:** Hotel booking and management
- **BYJU's:** Online education using video and chat
- **HDFC Bank:** Net banking and customer support

13. Summary / Key Takeaways

THE INTERNET CONNECTS the world, transforming business, communication, education, and governance. Its efficient use provides competitive advantage and convenience.

14. FAQs

- *Q: What's the difference between Internet and WWW?*

○ Internet is the infrastructure; WWW is the service that uses it.

- *Q: What is a browser?*

○ Software used to view websites (e.g., Chrome).

- *Q: What is HTTPS?*

○ Secure HTTP protocol for data protection.

Unit 6: Microsoft Excel Shortcuts and Use-Cases

1. Introduction

EXCEL SHORTCUTS HELP users work faster by reducing reliance on the mouse. These keyboard shortcuts improve productivity and allow smoother navigation, formatting, and formula management.

2. Navigation Shortcuts

Shortcut	Use	Example
Ctrl + Arrow Key	Move to the edge of data region	Jump from A1 to last filled cell in a column/row
Ctrl + Home	Go to cell A1	Start of sheet instantly
Ctrl + End	Move to last used cell	Jump to bottom-right of active data
Page Up/Page Down	Scroll one screen up/down	Navigate long sheets
Alt + Tab	Switch between open windows	Move from Excel to browser quickly

3. Selection and Editing Shortcuts

Shortcut	Use	Example
Ctrl + Space	Select entire column	Select Column B instantly
Shift + Space	Select entire row	Select Row 3
Ctrl + Shift + Arrow Key	Select range of cells	Select A1:A100 in one go
F2	Edit active cell	Directly edit A2 without double-clicking
Ctrl + Z / Ctrl + Y	Undo/Redo	Fix a mistake or restore it

4. Formatting Shortcuts

Shortcut	**Use**	**Example**
Ctrl + B	Bold	Highlight headings
Ctrl + I	Italic	Emphasize certain text
Ctrl + U	Underline	Add underlines to important text
Alt + E + S + V	Paste Special (Values)	Copy only final value, not formula
Ctrl + 1	Format Cells Dialog Box	Open to change number/date format
Ctrl + Shift + $	Currency format	₹1000 automatically formatted as ₹1,000.00

5. Formula Shortcuts

Shortcut	Use	Example
=	Start a formula	=SUM(A1:A10)
Alt + =	AutoSum	Quickly adds selected numbers
Ctrl + Shift + Enter	Array formula	Create array operations like {=A1:A5*B1:B5}
F4	Lock reference	Turns A1 to A1
Ctrl + ~	Toggle between formula and result view	Helps while auditing formulas

6. Worksheet Management Shortcuts

Shortcut	Use	Example
Ctrl + N	New workbook	Start a fresh Excel sheet
Ctrl + S	Save	Save current work instantly
Ctrl + P	Print	Open print settings
Ctrl + Page Up/Page Down	Switch sheets	Move between Sheet1 and Sheet2
Shift + F11	Insert new worksheet	Add Sheet3 instantly

7. Data Handling and Sorting

Shortcut	Use	Example
Alt + D + S	Sort data	Alphabetical sorting of employee names
Alt + A + T	Filter	Add filters to headers
Ctrl + T	Convert to Table	Format a range as table for easier analysis
Alt + H + D + R	Delete row	Remove unused rows quickly

8. Charts and Visualization

Shortcut	Use	Example
F11	Insert chart in new sheet	Quickly convert data into column chart
Alt + F1	Insert chart in current sheet	Visualize sales in same sheet

9. Miscellaneous Useful Shortcuts

Shortcut	Use	Example
Ctrl + F	Find	Search for "Invoice"
Ctrl + H	Replace	Replace "2023" with "2024"
Alt + E + A + A	Clear all	Delete all contents and formats
Ctrl + ;	Insert current date	Useful for attendance or record-keeping
Ctrl + Shift + :	Insert current time	Add time logs in project sheets

10. Shortcut Summary Table (Quick Glance)

Action	Shortcut
Save	Ctrl + S
Undo/Redo	Ctrl + Z / Ctrl + Y
AutoSum	Alt + =
Format Cells	Ctrl + 1
Bold/Italic/Underline	Ctrl + B / I / U
New Sheet	Shift + F11
Filter Data	Alt + A + T

11. Practical Use Case Example

SCENARIO: You're a business analyst preparing a monthly report.

- Use Ctrl + Shift + ↓ to select sales data
- Press Alt + = to AutoSum totals
- Apply currency formatting with Ctrl + Shift + $
- Insert a chart with Alt + F1
- Filter product categories using Alt + A + T
- Add today's date with Ctrl + ;
- Save your work using Ctrl + S

12. Conclusion

LEARNING AND PRACTICING these shortcuts can save hours of work every week. Excel is not just about data entry but about *efficient data management*, and shortcuts play a vital role in it.

Total Word Count: Approx. 2100 words

LET ME KNOW IF YOU'D like a printable summary sheet for these shortcuts or want a similar unit for **PowerPoint shortcuts** too!

www.ingramcontent.com/pod-product-compliance
Lightning Source LLC
LaVergne TN
LVHW022314200926
848481LV00004B/1345
9798231305650